the Lefty notebook

Where the Right Way to Write is Left!

RUNNING PRESS
PHILADELPHIA • LONDON

20 19 18 17 16 15 14 13
Digit on the right indicates the number of this printing.

ISBN-13 978-0-7624-0942-6
ISBN-10 0-7624-0942-8

Designed by Terry Peterson
Edited by Danielle McCole

This book may be ordered by mail from the publisher.
Please include $1.00 for postage and handling.
But try your bookstore first!

Running Press Book Publishers
2300 Chestnut Street
Philadelphia, Pennsylvania 19103-4371

Visit us on the web!
www.runningpress.com

Some left-handed resources:

Left Hand World, Inc.
Pier 39
San Francisco, California
Phone: (415) 433-3547

The Left Hand Supply Company
P.O. Box 20188
Oakland, California 94620
(510) 658-LEFT

On the Other Hand
6907 Woodtrail Ct.
Fort Wayne, Indiana 46835
phone: (219) 486-2702
fax: (219) 486-7428
WWW: http://www.ontheotherhand.com

Some Lefty Organizations:

League of Left-handers
Mike and Tom Geden
P.O. Box 495
Maple Shade, NJ 08052
e-mail: leagueoflefthanders@bigfoot.net

Sinistral SIG
200 Emmett Ave.
Derby, CT 06418
(203) 735-1759
This organization welcomes left-handed
people whose IQs are in the top 2 percent
of the population, and who are also eligible
to be members of Mensa.

Left Handers International
Ms. Nancy Campbell
Executive Director
3601 SW 29th Street
Topeka, KS 66614

Lefty, Inc.
P.O. Box 1054
Torrence, CA 90505

The Left-Handed Compliment
11359 Bolas Street
Los Angeles, CA 90049

"Left-handers have more enthusiasm for life."

—*Casey Stengel, Baseball coach*

If you sweep a broom left-handed, it's a good bet that you'll play golf better as a lefty.

Jimi Hendrix re-strung his guitar so that he could play it left-handed.

At any given time, approximately 40 percent of the top tennis pros are left-handed.

"Any Group that includes Charlemagne, Rock Hudson, Paul McCartney, Leonardo da Vinci, Benjamin Franklin, Jack the Ripper, and the Boston Strangler must be select, if not elite."

—Author James De Kay

"Labels are devices for saving talkative persons the trouble of thinking."
—*John Morley, writer*

We are taught to throw salt over our left shoulders in order to propitiate the fiends that are believed to always lurk to the left.

Recent studies show that 95 percent of fetuses
in the womb suck their right thumb and 5 percent
suck their left.

St. Lawrence University performed a study in 1989 which found no correlation between left-handedness and birth order.

Left-handed falsehood: Left-handedness is a neurotic choice made by anti-social individuals.

Lefties even tend to tie their shoelaces differently.
Left-handers generally cross first with the left lace on top
of the right lace, then form the first loop to the right.

"Most important, we want society to realize that left-handers have special needs and shouldn't be forced to conform to the world of right-handers."

—*Jancy Campbell, Executive Director of Left-handers International*

If the left side of the body is controlled by the

right side of the brain, then left-handed people

are the only ones in their right minds.

Left-handed children are two to three times more likely to suffer from juvenile diabetes.

Lefties tend to have a better memory for music than right-handers.

"Right handers are a bunch of chocolate soldiers.
If you've seen one, you've seen 'em all."

—*Dr. Joseph Bogan, Neurosurgeon*

Methods as extreme as tying a child's left
arm down were often used to force
them into right-handedness.

"Lefty" Grove, considered by some to be the greatest baseball pitcher of all time, worked miracles for the Philadelphia Athletics in the 1920s and 1930s.

No one really knows what causes someone to be left-handed or right-handed.

A few things that make life for a lefty a little more difficult:

Playing cards
Aprons
Butter knives
Watch stems
Ice cream scoops
Slot machines

The saying, "offer your left hand in friendship," actually means to stab one in the back.

Both words "awkward" and "gawky" come from
the word *awke*, meaning "from the left."

Lefty by other names:

molly-dukers: (Australian) molly meaning effeminate, and dukers referring to hands

pen-pushers: (English) as many left handers have to push the pen across the paper while writing

Portsiders: based on the port side of the ship

In general, being left-handed means having a dominant right side of the brain.

"When I was a kid, I seemed to do everything back to front."
—*Paul McCartney, Singer*

James Michener, who was right-handed, often mistakenly appears on lists of famous lefties.

M.C. Escher attributed his decision to become a graphic artist,
rather than a painter, to his left-handedness.

"All left-handed people feel awkward, but they think they're clumsy when actually they don't have the proper tools."

—June Gittleson, proprietor of The Left Hand, a specialty store in New York

Ramses II was always shown to be left-handed.

Older mothers are more likely to have left-handed children than younger mothers.

The lefty tendency to be impulsive helped left-handed Joan of Arc succeed in battle.

Psychologist Abram Blau held the opinion that left-handers were simply anti-social and used the "wrong" hand just to be troublemakers.

Left-handed falsehood: Left-handedness is the result of poor toilet training.

There is an unusually high incidence of left-handedness in fraternal
twins. However, it is rare for both to be left-handed.

Between 15 and 30 percent of all patients in mental institutions are left-handed.

"I would have to sign autographs with my hand up in the air like the body of a tarantula."

—*Cloris Leachman, Actress*

United States Senator Robert Dole became

left-handed after a combat injury in Italy

crippled his right hand.

Left-handed falsehood: All people are born right-handed. Some become left-handed because they are mentally or physically deficient.

Some famous left-handed criminals:

Jack the Ripper
Billy the Kid
The Boston Strangler
John Dillinger

"It's a crying shame that 10 percent of the world's
population has to go through life backward."

—*Christopher Mills, Entrepreneur*

"We're crazy as a species if we try to push everybody through the same cookie mold."

—Jerry Levy

Handwriting is one of the most difficult motor control tasks; this is why handedness is usually determined by the hand with which you write.

One U.S. study shows that blondes are twice as likely to be left-handed as redheads or brunets.

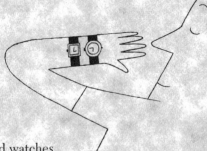

Timex produces two different models of left-handed watches.

Some top-selling items at Left-Handed World in San Francisco:

Left-handed scissors
Left-handed corkscrews
Left-handed can openers

While only 10 percent of the population is left-handed, 20 percent of MENSA, the high-I.Q. society, is left-handed.

"The key to a hockey fight is the first punch. When you're a lefty, they're looking for the right. It helps."

—*Wayne Cashman, hockey player and coach*

Some traits that are associated with lefties:

Less rigid
More artistic
More sensual
Less controlling

Left handers are faster and more adept to typing
and word processing than right handers.

Some famous left-handed musicians:

Bob Dylan
Carl Philipp Emanuel Bach
Cristal Gayle
Paul McCartney
Ludwig van Beethoven
Jimi Hendrix

It has been estimated that left-handers are
eleven times more likely to be dyslexic than
right-handers.

"It is better to stand on the wrong side of
the ball, and hit it right, than to stand on the
right side of the ball, and hit it wrong."

—*Motto of the National Association of
Left-Handed Golfers*

In 1891, the term "southpaw" was coined by a Chicago sportswriter to describe left-handed baseball pitchers. Because of the way that some old ballparks were situated, pitchers faced west: thus, a left-handed pitcher's pitching arm was to the south.

The *New England Journal of Medicine* suggests that you can tell if you're left-handed if the base of your left thumbnail is wider and squarer than your right.

Why do we wear our wedding bands on the third finger of the left hand?

The custom dates back to the early Egyptian belief that the *vena amoris* (vein of love) ran directly from the heart to the third finger of the left hand.

"I can see a day when a 90-degree angle is known as a 'left' angle; when a moral, virtuous person will be called 'lefteous'; and when a box standing on its bottom will be 'up-left'."

—Customer at Westport specialty shop

There was even a time in Japan when mere left-handedness in a wife was sufficient ground for expelling her.

Left-handed tennis players are said to play
a "wristier" game, as they tend to put
more spin on their serves.

Brooks Robinson, the great Oriole third baseman, batted and threw right-handed, but he signed autographs with his left hand.

If both parents are left-handed, there is a 50 percent chance that their children will be.

"I always felt special being left-handed. I always thought it was a special gift. I figured all sensitive and creative people were left-handed."

—*Susan Rios, Artist*

Some famous left-handed writers:

Jean Genet
Mark Twain
Bernadette de Wit
Lewis Carroll
Dave Barry
Peter Benchley

Though Albert Einstein wrote and played violin with his right hand, he is listed as a famous lefty. This is because he displays many of the characteristics of a "switched" left-hander.

In most cases, left-handed people can read backward better than right-handed people.

Lefties have a better recovery rate from severe hand injuries than righties.

There was a time when Native Americans
were the largest single population
of lefties: one in every three.

Why are there more left-handed males than females?

Scientists have speculated that an excessive level of
testosterone slows the development of the left side
of the brain, which allows the right side of the brain
to achieve and maintain dominance.

If both parents are right-handed, a mere 2 percent of their children will be left-handed.

August 13th has been designated as International Left-handers Day.

One out of every four Apollo astronauts was left-handed.

Bowling shoes are "handed" by the type of sole that is on the sliding shoe. Since (most) left-handed bowlers slide with their right foot, the right shoe is soled with some type of leather or buckskin to aid in sliding.

Scotland harbors many mysteries, including a clan that is believed to have had an unusually high proportion of left-handers: the clan Kerr. This belief is so deeply engrained in Scotland that corry-fisted and Kerr-handed have become common Scottish synonyms for left-handed.

Some famous left-handed basketball greats:

Digger Phelps
Bill Russell
Larry Bird
Charles "Lefty" Driesell
Walter Berry
Dick Motta

Some famous left-handed football greats:

Steve Young
Jim Zorn
Terry Baker
Norman "Boomer" Esiason
Bobby Douglass
Paul McDonald

Honeysuckle is one of the few plants that are "left-handed," as it twines to the left as it climbs.

The word "sinister" is almost verbatim the Latin word for left-handed.

Some famous left-handed performers:

Julia Roberts
Lenny Bruce
Diane Keaton
Joanne Woodward
Pierce Brosnan
Danny Kaye

There is speculation that the one group that is dominantly left-handed is gorillas, as their left arms tend to outweigh their right, suggesting a left-handed bias.

The Incas believe that left-handedness was a sign of luck.

It is against the rules of polo to play left-handed.

Left-handed places in the United States:

Lefthand Bay, Alaska
Left Cape, Arkansas
Lefthand Luman Creek, Wyoming

Left-handed people adjust more readily to underwater vision.

Arguably, 2 to 30 percent of any human population

is left-handed or ambidextrous, with most estimates

hovering around 10 percent, depending upon the

criteria used to assess handedness.

One of the few things that favors lefties are tollbooths.

In the 1900s, American writer and educator A.N. Palmer held symposiums across the country explaining that left-handed children should be forced to be right-handed. His rationale was that it was a right-handed world, and that children must be taught the value of conformity.

Left-handed people are believed to be
intuitive, mystical, and strongly visual.
This is due to the fact that they use
the "feeling" side of their brain more
than right-handed people.

In classic tarot cards, Justice is depicted as right-handed and the Devil as left-handed.

"I'm sure it's not just chance that Pablo Picasso, Michelangelo, Leonardo da Vinci, and a long list of other artists have all been left-handed or ambidextrous."

—Dr. Jeanine Herron,
research psychologist in neuropsychiatry

Inuits believe that all left-handed people are potential sorcerers.

Among the presidents of the United States of America, there have been an unusually high number of left-handers—about one in every three. But in the 1992 elections, there was not even a right-handed *candidate*. Both the incumbent president Bush and his rivals Clinton and Ross Perot were left-handers.

Left-handers are roughly twice as likely to have a lefthanded child as right-handers.

That is all there is left to say.